The Distance Between Names

Mehar Arora

BookLeaf
Publishing

India | USA | UK

Made with ❤ on the BookLeaf Publishing Platform

www.bookleafpub.in

www.bookleafpub.com

Dedication

for my mother, who gave me stories before I had words,
who saw a poet in every question I asked,
and gave me a voice stitched from hers.

Preface

These poems began with small murmurs- fragments of thought that bloomed in the quiet corners of my mind. They are made of moments I almost forgot, of softness I took for weakness and for love that never left, even when everything else did.

I have always believed that stories arrive before words do - in small gestures, glances, or even the way someone says your name. Daisies became a symbol of this collection. Not just because of their beauty, but their persistence. They grow in thei unlikelist places, quietly, bravely, without asking to be noticed. In many ways, i think that's what healing looks like.

Because poetry , like love, is rarely about understanding, it's about *feelings seen.*

Acknowledgements

to my father, the first man i ever loved.

to my brother, for being my mirror & my compass.

*to my friends, who never asked me to explain my
silences.*

*& to champ, whose paws no longer touch this world but
whose joy still echoes in every open field.*

1. In the Quiet, He stays

My monsters feast when the night turns still,
They gnaw at my thoughts, bend my will.
Shadows of fear, they creep and play,
Yet somehow, he makes it all go away.

Without a word, he calms the storm,
His silence wraps me, safe and warm.
There's something in the quiet he keeps,
That lulls my chaos and soothes my weeps.

He loves the praise, and I love to give.
A balance of hearts in the lives we live.
He listens to cricket, though it's not his game,
Yet in his eyes, I see no blame.

We argue, we laugh, we tease and jest,
But when he says "chill," my heart finds rest.
It's magic, I swear, the way he speaks,
Even in silence, he finds what I seek.

And if you're out there, listening to this,
Know that your absence is a bitter abyss.
I miss you like crazy, my days feel grey,
And I long for your hug when I'm back someday.

So here's my hope, whispered to the air,
That you're okay and beyond despair.
Because with you, my nightmares cease,
You are my calm, my quiet, my peace.

2. The Almost Lovers

I loved the wrong ones, time after time,
The ones with ties that weren't to me,
Their eyes, their words, a tempting rhyme—
But they were songs of longing, not to be.

I chased shadows under borrowed moons,
Held hands with ghosts in crowded rooms,
Watched smiles fall like passing tunes,
Brief, then gone—sweet but doomed.

And then there's you, with kindness fierce,
Who looks at me like I might be home,
Your laugh so warm, your gaze so clear,
Yet I know in truth, your heart still roams.

You do the things that lovers do,
You say the things I wish were true,
But between us lies a secret ache,
A bridge that neither of us will take.

I loved the wrong ones, and now I see—
This pattern is drawn like waves to shore,
The heart I want is never free,
And the ones who are, I can't adore.

So I'll watch you drift, as lovers do,
Each tethered to our separate stars,
And though my heart will burn for you,
I'll let it learn to heal its scars.

3. The Weight of Love

Love's been a funny thing to me,
A thread of hope, too light to see.
I gave my all to him, my first,
The one I thought could quench my thirst.
He was perfect—my parents' dream,
But life's not always what it seems.
Two years of love, but twice betrayed,
His lies are scars that never fade.
Unforgivable, yet so profound,
He left me shattered on the ground.

Then came another, full of care,
A heart too big for me to bear.
He loved me more than I could feel,
But my heart stayed locked, the pain too real.
Two days were all it took to part,
While he's still lost inside his heart.
I moved on quickly, but he held tight,
Still hoping for another fight.
He deserved more than I could give,

In the shadows of the past, I live.

Two years passed, my heart turned cold,
Love's warm embrace felt tired, old.
But then he came, a gentle flame,
And though we never played love's game,
He calmed the storm, my raging sea,
And in his eyes, I found some peace.
I regret the things we couldn't be,
The chances lost, the "what ifs" are free.
He never knew how deep it went,
The love I gave, the time I spent.

They say I love too many boys,
That I play hearts just like toys.
But they don't know the love I hide,
The way it burns so fiercely inside.
When I love, I love so wild,
Not some fleeting, careless child.
Maybe that's why it's never me,
Why does love slip through so easily?
I give too much, I fall too fast,
And always wonder why it passed.

But one day, love will meet its match,
And someone won't just light a match—
They'll stand beside me, face the waves,

And love me through the stormy days.
Until then, I'll love like fire,
A raging heart, a burning pyre.

4. 20 Days

His voice once whispered peace to me,
A calm that set my heartbeats free.
He'd say my name with nothing more,
Yet in that silence, I'd adore.

I'd watch him walk, my heart would race,
Like thunder pounding in its place.
His eyes they held my hopes so bright,
His touch, a promise wrapped in light.

But now those dreams belong to her,
The hope I held is now a blur.
The peace he gave has slipped away,
Into her arms, where I can't stay.

I see her crawl back to his side,
Despite the hurt, despite the pride.
I wonder if she values her worth,
But then I think, I'd do the same on earth.

That August Friday broke my soul,
The pain, the loss, beyond control.
But now the hurt has started to fade,
Though memories of him still invade.

In six months, when he is gone,
This chapter's end will carry on.
And while it's true, he'll soon forget,
I hope that by then I won't regret it.

His voice once held the weight of care,
His texts were promises laid bare.
His eyes, they painted futures bright,
His touch, a world that felt just right.

But now that world is hers to hold,
The promises that once felt bold.
And though I'd take him back again,
I know it's all in vain.

Yet here I stand, still thinking why,
I'd let him in, despite the lie.
But now, that ache has started to cease,
That storm within is finding peace.

The tears I shed on that dark day,
Don't haunt me quite the same today.

And when he leaves, I'll let him go,
Time will heal what I now know.

He was the one, my hope, my light,
But now it's fading from my sight.
I lived for the dreams he used to give,
But now, without him, I will live.

"What's meant for you will find its way,
What's not will surely go astray."
And in that truth, I'll find my calm,
No longer reaching for his palm.

5. A Smile that Breaks Me

Every day it's your smile that catches me,
draws me back to a fleeting sunset that I rarely see.
the way your smile lines shine,
It's where my world resides
a small secret I keep, not knowing my heart collides.

I sit alone at night, searching for your voice in the
shadows
that warmth and comfort of your voice, while the wind
blows
I hold every memory close to my heart-
knowing that one day it'll be all distant, like dreams that
never start

It's always somebody else
And never me, I've told myself.
I laugh at your jokes, hold you when you cry- it's just a
mask that I wear.
Inside hides an ache I'll never dare to share.

But it's okay, as long as you stay
even in stolen glances, never really knowing what to say.
And as much as it hurts, I can never let go
, for your smile is the only comfort I know.

6. Monsters?

They told me the monsters lived under my bed,
hid in the dark, waiting, filling me with dread.
But no one warned me they'd wear a kind face,
smile like home, then take its place.

I walked through a crime scene painted in trust,
never seeing the footprints left in the dust.
The whispers, the hands, the shadows that grew,
One by one, they took all that I knew.

My laughter, my love, the friends that I made,
gone in a blink, in a game that they played.
Now she wears my life like a dress she once stole,
and I stand here empty, a body without soul.

And maybe, just maybe, I think of that night,
when my mother once told me to fear what's in sight.
Not under my bed, not deep in my head—
But the ones who walk near me whisper instead.

Even the prince couldn't save the princess this time, for the monsters weren't hiding—they walked in the light.

7. The Dance You Didn't Choose

I bite my tongue, swallow the ache,
Hide the cracks that threaten to break.
I won't show you the hurt inside,
For my love is quiet, my pain denied.

You tread softly, afraid to wound,
Guarding your past like a sacred tune.
I understand—your heart's in two,
But do you see what I gave you?

I left my world, my walls, my pride,
To stand with you, by your side.
But the smallest things, they tear me apart,
For they're not small when they reach my heart.

It's not the dance, not the step, not the song,
But the choice of someone else all along.
With her, you danced without a care,
But with me, it's as if you're not there.

I ache for a love that's wholly mine,
Not a shadow that lingers through time.
I gave you all, yet here I stand,
Hoping you'll one day understand.

It's not just the steps, the music, the chance—
It's about the person you choose to dance with.
And though I ache, I'll never demand,
I just hope you'll take my hand.

8. Final Let Go

I let him go with hands unclasped,
No final words, no painful gasp.
Not mourning him, not wishing back,
Yet flashbacks hit like cracks in glass.

Two months ago, I wore that smile,
The one she has now for a while.
I stood beside him, felt that rush,
Believed in love, let down my hush.

For two long years, I guarded tight,
My heart locked up, kept out of sight.
But he found cracks within the wall,
I let myself believe and fall.

He said he couldn't stay or fight,
Yet still he did, in someone's light.
He promised her what I once craved
Commitment, something I had saved.

Though deep inside, I know the truth,
That fleeting love will meet its proof.
But seeing him now give his word
Hurts like a song you've always heard.

It's not that I would take him back,
I've no regrets, no missing track.
But knowing he could give away
What I once wanted makes me sway.

And now there's someone new who stirs
The feelings are long ignored or blurred.
I wonder if he'll be the same,
A spark that fades into the flame.

I pray he's different, holds my hand,
Stays with me longer than the sand.
I hope he's real, not just a phase,
Not just another heart to chase.

I let him go, with steady breath,
Yet echoes linger in his stead.
But someone new stands in my view,
And maybe this time, he'll be true.

9. November 3rd

He walks with grace, quiet and kind,
A giver of light, though shadows unwind.
His heart beats not for himself alone,
But for others, their burdens he makes his own.

He battles his demons, unseen, unsaid,
A war within the walls of his head.
No cry for help, no sign of strife,
He carries it all, the weight of life.

Each step he takes is toward something more,
A better version, a brighter shore.
In his dance, I see his soul take flight,
Expression of struggle turned into light.

If only he knew the care that surrounds,
The love that lingers, the warmth that abounds.
His strength inspires, his courage awes,
Yet his own worth is the one he withdraws.

To him, I'd whisper if he'd let me near:
"You matter more than you may appear.
Your giving heart deserves its rest,
For you, too, deserve to feel your best."

He hides his pain, but I see it still,
The silent hero with an iron will.
If only he'd pause and let it show,
That the love he gives has room to grow.

10. Oh no, I'm falling again.

It starts like a whisper, soft and low,
A flutter inside where shadows grow.
A spark rekindled, long thought gone,
Awakens the heart to a brand-new dawn.

I see you there, a vision, a light,
Your presence turning the day to night.
Every glance, a brush of fire,
Ignites a long-forgotten desire.

I crave your voice, your laugh, your stare,
The moments we share, so light, so rare.
But when you're gone, the silence screams,
And pulls me deeper into dreams.

Yet fear lingers, a shadow near,
Whispering doubts that I don't want to hear.
What if you don't feel the same?
What if I'm left with only the flame?

Still, your beauty feels like home,
A place my soul dares not roam.
I hate the thought of being apart,
For you've already claimed my fragile heart.

So here I stand, trembling, bare,
Hoping you'll see what's written there.
Not just longing, but love untold,
A story waiting to unfold.

But if this falls, and pain takes its place,
I'll hold on to this fleeting grace.
For even the ache is worth the chance,
Of catching your eye, of one fleeting dance.

11. Uncharted Distance

I know I can't hold what isn't mine,
Yet here we stand, toeing the line.
You say her name, and I feel the space—
A girl far away, a truth I can't chase.

We walk like lovers, side by side,
Share hidden glances we both deny.
A whisper, a laugh, that secret spark,
Lighting up what should stay dark.

I see the pull, I feel the weight,
The silent wish, the patient waits.
In almost every, every near,
A half-formed love I can't make clear.

You're tethered still, I see the thread—
A bond that stretches but doesn't shed.
And here I am, just close enough
To taste the ache, to crave the touch.

I know it's wrong, I feel it's right,
This hollow dance in borrowed light.
We orbit close, we draw and drift,
Bound to a love we'll never lift.

12. The Stages of Love

Infatuation
It starts with sparks, a passing glance,
A heart caught up in a newfound trance.
They walk your way, your senses thrill—
Infatuation strikes at will.

Attraction
Now drawn like tides, you feel the sway,
In every smile, you drift away.
The pull is strong, you can't ignore—
Attraction knocks upon your door.

Friendship
Then words flow soft, like whispered streams,
You share your thoughts, confess your dreams.
They're there for you, no mask, no guise—
In friendship, trust and laughter rise.

Feelings

A brush of hands, a careful pause,
You're lost in moments just because.
Your heartbeat stirs, emotions wake,
As feelings bloom for both to take.

Connection
You're intertwined, a silent dance,
Each glance speaks more than words by chance.
Together now, as two hearts blend,
Connection forms, two souls to mend.

Obsession
But love grows fierce, intense, unbound,
They're all you seek; the world spins round.
Their voice, their steps, your constant need—
Obsession plants its endless seed.

Loss
And then, at last, comes love's retreat,
An empty ache, a rhythm beat.
The tether snaps, the light withdraws—
Loss whispers in the pause.

Each stage of a story, bold yet frail,
The journey of love, its endless tale.

13. So Quick

A month and five days, that's all it took,
For him to turn a page, close the book.
Not on their story, but on mine—
It's funny how love can shift with time.

He said he "loved" me once, so sweet,
But now, those words feel incomplete.
Love, for him, comes like the breeze,
Whispered promises, gone with ease.

They're dating now—his hand in hers,
While I'm left counting the past in blurs.
It's not their smiles or tender grace,
But the emptiness in the space we'd trace.

And then, he removed me from his feed,
Maybe that's the proof I didn't need.
Maybe that's how he shows he'll stay—
Commit to her differently.

Perhaps this time he'll really try,
Maybe this love won't be a lie.
Perhaps for her, he'll be what he wasn't for me,
And they'll grow into something I couldn't foresee.

And honestly, I hope they work out fine,
I hope their hearts are more in line.
I wish them well, with all my heart,
As I stand alone, torn apart.

14. Sailor

I saw him again today, like I do every day,
In his red house t-shirt, catching the morning's sway.
It took me back to that Friday, the one I can't forget,
The day it ended—our love, a dream unmet.

He said he didn't want to give love a chance,
But here he stands, lost in someone else's glance.
I'm genuinely happy, that's what I'll always say,
But why does it hurt when she's the one, not me, today?

Her blue house t-shirt matches his red just fine,
And I wonder, in another world, could that have been
mine?
But I'll never break the bond they now seem to share,
Even though every look at them is more than I can bear.

I won't ruin what they've started to build,
I'll step aside, though it leaves me unfulfilled.

I'll watch from afar as they grow hand in hand,
My heart breaks silently, but I'll still withstand.

My friends—they hate him, their anger's like fire,
But it doesn't extinguish my quiet desire.
They ache when they see me cry every night,
But they don't know how real it felt when it was right.

August slipped away, leaving nothing but scars,
It took him with it, leaving me chasing stars.
I hate to admit how much I still care,
But I care more for her, and that's my silent prayer.

15. deja vu

I want to let you go, it's clear,
But memories of you still linger near.
We spent those days, though far too few,
In laughter, in talks that felt so true.

Do you remember the nights we shared?
Under the stars, where no one cared
About the world beyond our sight,
Just you and I, in whispered light.

We walked for miles, no end in view,
And in each step, I fell for you.
But there was a hug that never came,
A moment lost, we're both to blame.

I wanted to reach out, to pull you close,
But fear kept me locked, like a fading ghost.
And so, we drifted, day by day,
Until you found another way.

A month passed by in a blink,
In solitude, I'd sit and think
Of what we were and what we'd be,
If only you had chosen me.

I hold the past, but not too tight,
For in my heart, there's a new light.
I've found the strength to love again,
But you'll always be a lingering when.

16. Just A Call?

You called her.
The one i begged you not to look at twice.
the one whose name clung to my insecurity
like a perfume I could never wash off.
the one you said meant nothing—
over and over
until I let myself believe you.
You called her
not in rage, not in chaos,
but in the soft, secret hour
when men make decisions they pretend are harmless.
And when did it become so easy
to talk about me with the girl I was afraid of?
Was it before or after you kissed my forehead
and said,
"I'm not that guy"?
I wonder if she sounded familiar,
like a memory you didn't want to let go of.
I wonder if she laughed
when you said things with your chest

that you never dared to say to my face.
Did she feel like home
while I was busy building one around you?
I didn't know.
for a whole month.
I kissed you, I called you,
I told my friends,
"he's really trying this time."
But it turns out I was just background music
while you flipped to a chapter
you swore you'd closed.
and now you dance with her world again—
through her friend, through freshers,
through the echo of everything you said was over
I watch from across the room.
eyes dry, stomach in knots,
heart whispering:
Don't do it, don't *miss* him.
But it's not that simple.
You weren't handsome.
You weren't popular.
You were just...
there.
And somehow that was enough
for me to throw myself into belief
that maybe love isn't always shiny.
Maybe it's just being seen.

But you saw me
in a dim light,
only when it was convenient.
You heard me say no,
more than once—
and paused like it was a choice.
So no,
this isn't just heartbreak.
This is grief laced with anger,
confusion tangled in old softness.
this is wanting to scream and kiss you in the same
breath,
to shake you and say,
"Do you even *get* what you lost?"
But I won't.
I can't.
Because if I speak to you now,
I might forget what you did.
I might fold again
under the weight of your guilt,
mistake it for love,
and lose myself one more time.
And I'm done losing myself.
not for someone
who was just there.

17. Wish I Hated You.

I wish I hated you.
I wish your name didn't taste like sweetness caught in a
lie,
like comfort that turned cold in my hands
While I kept calling it warmth.
I loved you louder than you deserved—
more honest, more whole.
I held your tiredness when you left me crying on calls,
I stitched your self-doubt with my dreams,
and you...
You told me not to worry about her.
her.
the one who lived behind your reassurances,
the one you called when I thought we were healing,
the one you made me feel small next to
while you swore you weren't looking back.
And now you dance with her world,
like you never stood in mine.
Like I didn't kiss you with all the parts of me
that believed love could fix you.

I don't hate you.

That's the worst part.

Some part of me still wants to fold into your chest,

ask why you didn't just tell me the truth.

some part of me still sees the version of you i made in

my head—

gentle, brave, worth it.

But now I know better.

Guilt is easy.

growth is not.

And your sorrys can't unkiss the betrayal,

can't unspeak the lies you dressed in comfort.

I deserve more than someone

who only loves me in the spaces

where it's convenient.

So I won't slap you.

I won't hug you.

I will carry this ache like a fire

that one day stops burning me

and starts lighting my way.

and if we meet again,

know—

I loved you more than you knew what to do with.

But I'm learning now

how to love myself even more.

18. October's Lessons

Every October, love finds its start
each year- directly into my heart.
three men, three stories, three different ways.
swept away in the golden October haze.

the first, a love that burned oh so right-
Two years of trust were shattered one night.
Whispers of betrayal where promises once lay
taught me to guard myself and never give away.

The second, perhaps a one-sided tale,
just a dream - a story that couldn't prevail.
It was just a few weeks of smiles and hope
ended without a reason, like it never had any scope.

the third, the one where I left no strings unturned
Two hearts danced, but one never aligned.
I learnt that a love that moves on fast, even unmet,

leaves a scar and nobody can forget.

I have always been the poet, crafting my songs-
hoping someday, somebody would sing-along.
October, you keeper of heartbreaks and dreams-
Teach me again, though my love rarely redeems.

19. You Were Bigger Than The Whole Sky

I didn't lash out to cause you pain,
Just tired of silence, tired of strain.
I asked for time, respect, a voice—
Not guilt or games, just an honest choice.
You juggle life, I understand,
But still I offered you my hand.
Yet every time I tried to care,
You made me feel I wasn't there.
You called it casual, played it cool,
But kindness isn't breaking rules.
You say you're busy, always tired—
Then why respond once things get dire?
I wasn't rude, I wasn't cold,
But damn, your tone was far too bold.
Not friends, not now—that much is true,
'Cause friends don't treat each other blue.
You got your match, your team, your game,
Congrats—no spite, I feel no shame.
But when I reached out just to try,

You brushed me off, no reason why.
I wrote, I paused, I waited long,
But silence told me I was wrong.
So here's the last thing I will send,
No need to patch, no need to mend.
I'll mail your things, I'll let you go,
No grudge, just truth you didn't show.
You wanted space, I gave you air—
But I deserved a little care.
So keep your wins, your match, your pride—
I'll walk alone, but dignified.
You taught me what I shouldn't be,
And now I'm choosing to be free.

20. The Game of Bat & Ball

You stand at the crease,
eyes steady, smile somewhere between courage and
calm.
The afternoon hums —
crowds fade, and it's just you and the rhythm of breath.
I watch the ball rise,
curving like a promise in slow motion.
You swing —
and for a second, time forgets to move.
Love feels like that, doesn't it?
A shot that finds the gap,
a risk you take knowing
It might all end in the hands of a fielder —
and yet, you play,
because the sound of leather meeting heart
It is worth everything.

21. It's a Goodbye.

It's been almost four months since we drifted apart,
The ache has faded, just a soft scar on my heart.
You moved on quickly, found someone new,
And now she's your trophy, your proof, your view.

I don't feel that same pang when I see you now,
No jealousy lingers; I don't ask how.
I lost a lot in loving you hard and deep,
But I've gained back those parts I thought I couldn't
keep.

I'm thriving alone, getting grades, earning praise,
While you flash your new life in polished displays.
I sometimes wonder what might have been,
But August slipped away like a summer scene.

So here's to moving on, to growing and grace,
To find myself in my own solid place.
You're a memory, now blurred and kind,
I'm finally free, with no past left to find.

www.ingramcontent.com/pod-product-compliance
Lightning Source LLC
Chambersburg PA
CBHW070038070426
42449CB00012BA/3086